Master Built Pools & Patios

An Inspiring Portfolio of Design Ideas

Tina Skinner

Schiffer Publishing Ltd

4880 Lower Valley Road, Atglen, PA 19310 USA

Library of Congress Cataloging-in-Publication Data

Skinner, Tina.
Master built pools & patios : an inspiring partfolio of design ideas /
Tina Skinner.
p. cm.
ISBN 0-7643-1747-4 (Hardcover)
1. Swimming pools. 2. Water gardens. I. Title: Master built pools and
patios. II. Title.
TH4763 .S57 2003
728'.96--dc21
2002012598

Cover page: Courtesy of Shasta Pools & Spas
Title page: ©Alan Gilbert Photography
Copyright page: Courtesy of Shasta Pools & Spas
Endsheets: Courtesy of New Bern Pool

Designed by Bonnie M. Hensley
Cover design by Bruce M. Waters
Type set in Swiss 911 UCm BT/Aldine 721 BT

ISBN: 0-7643-1747-4
Printed in China

Published by Schiffer Publishing Ltd.
4880 Lower Valley Road
Atglen, PA 19310
Phone: (610) 593-1777; Fax: (610) 593-2002
E-mail: info@schifferbooks.com
Please visit our web site catalog at **www.schifferbooks.com**
We are always looking for people to write books on new and related
subjects. If you have an idea for a book please contact us at the above
address.

This book may be purchased from the publisher. Include $3.95 for
shipping. Please try your bookstore first. You may write for a free catalog.

In Europe, Schiffer books are distributed by
Bushwood Books
6 Marksbury Ave.
Kew Gardens
Surrey TW9 4JF England
Phone: 44 (0) 20 8392-8585; Fax: 44 (0) 20 8392-9876
E-mail: Bushwd@aol.com
Free postage in the U.K., Europe; air mail at cost.

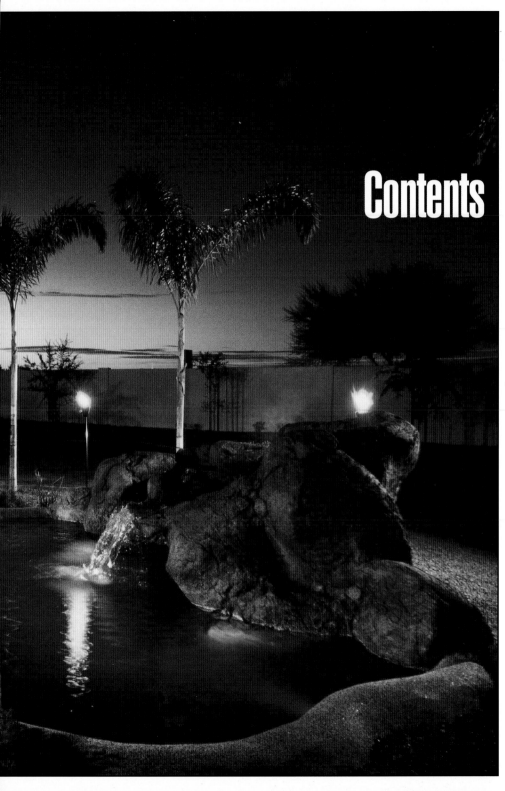

Contents

Acknowledgments

MASTER POOLS®

All books should be such a pleasure to do. Dick Covert and Ron Coker of the Master Pools Guild were all over the slightest suggestion that we might work together to create a beautiful book. In fact, it was only a matter of days until the membership had been rounded up and given orders to select their finest images and turn them over. It has been a true pleasure to work with this group – truly masters of their trade, and all eager to show off their work. After all, with the exception of the homeowners, it's the lucky guest who is invited into the backyard to view these masterpieces. The guild membership opens the gates for us, offering this grand tour of truly wonderful water works. Many thanks to all the members, even those who didn't make the deadline. We'll get you in the next book!

Stephen Foery has also been invaluable in seeing this project through to completion. He helped organize members and information, checked facts, and applied his own creative eye to the design and layout of this book.

Preface

The Master Pools Guild is proud to have the opportunity to contribute to this book and to display the crest that is our trademark. The crest of the Master Pools Guild is more than just a trademark. It is a symbol. The swimming pool builder who displays this crest is part of an elite group of the finest craftsmen in the world. For more than four decades, the Master Pools Guild has admitted only those builders who have demonstrated proven business ethics combined with superior design and building talents. Only those who consistently maintain those standards are permitted to remain as members. The crest of the Master Pools Guild is truly "The Mark Of Legendary Craftsmanship".

Every member of the Guild is dedicated to our customer's satisfaction and confidence. We believe that all pools should be designed to blend aesthetically with the natural surroundings combined with creative ideas to create the best possible backyard environment. Whether the pool is the focal point for family activities, business entertainment, a year round vacation venue for the family, or for a lifetime of health and fitness, a Master Pool is the answer!

Building a pool starts with careful planning and is an important financial investment in your home. Consideration must be given to the shape of the lot, the existing landscape, the terrain and the maximum sun exposure. Other considerations are lifestyle, entertainment needs, safety, budget and the likes and dislikes of the potential pool owner.

A Master Pools Guild member incorporates the latest technology and equipment in all the pools and spas they build. This technology allows the pool owner to control lighting, temperature, and water features such as fountains and waterfalls from a control system located inside the residence. We use only the finest filtration systems, heating systems and chemical control systems in the industry. All these factors are important in creating the proper pool environment that is both an asset and a source of pleasure to the owner for years to come.

Whatever you can imagine we can bring to focus. Whether you desire a lap pool for exercise, a natural setting with waterfalls, a family entertainment center, or a breathtaking vanishing edge pool, a Master Pools Guild builder can make your dreams come true.

On behalf of all Master Pools Guild members we sincerely hope you enjoy this publication and trust that you will watch for future books involving Master Pools and Spas.

Sincerely,

Ronald C. Coker, Sr.
Chairman of the Board

Courtesy of Shasta Pools & Spas

Introduction

Given a week of vacation and change to spare, most people are inclined to head down from the hills and gather on the shores of lakes, seas, and oceans. Water is the ultimate lure, be it to bathe or simply to soak in the sight of sparkly blue waters and the magical reflection of sunlight. One week a year seems a paltry allowance of this great pleasure, and so those who can build their own "cement pond" in the backyard.

This book illustrates just how elegant that concrete swimming hole can be. Functional, too. Bubbling hot spas can be incorporated into the swimming area, waterfalls can cascade into them, creating the soothing sound of falling water, and entire pool edges can be turned into endless, horizon-free cascades. Automatic covers can be designed to smoothly and safely seal off a pool. Or an entire addition might be built to house it. Some people choose to build a simple, narrow lane for athletic laps or to install poolside jets that create a workout area where you can swim your heart out — in place.

While some people design pools to imitate a natural pond, others might create a formal black reflecting pool to mirror their handsome home or pavilion. They might dedicate an acre to the site, creating a separate pool house, eating and cooking areas, a fireplace, and patio or seating that add up to an entire outdoor room. Decorative concrete applications, brick work, mosaics, and fieldstone may be incorporated to add beauty. Landscaping around the pool and patio can make it feel as though one is swimming in Paradise. The possibilities are endless, and that's just what this book illustrates.

Aesthetically, master pool builders work to create a pool that complements a home's architecture and landscaping. A well-thought out pool and patio appear as part of the master plan, devised by the lay of the land and the architect. When properly designed and installed, a pool adds to the value of the home at resale time. More importantly, though, it adds to the quality of life for those who live there.

Members of the Master Pools Guild are part of an elite group of craftsman, often second or third generation pool builders. They gather to create both a social and technical network, meeting for fellowship and to share technical accomplishments and stories about the finest homes and swimming holes in the world. In this book they share their accomplishments with a larger group, and we the readers are grateful.

Courtesy of Lifetime Pools, Inc.

© Jerry Buscher, PLP Portraits

9

Geometric Simplicity

The stereotypical pool is a rectangle, sloping on the bottom from shallow to deep-end. However, such a description defies the beauty that can be built into and around such a configuration. Once freed from simple rectangular bounds, the possibilities for straight-line design are endless.

The classic pool, a rectangle with a deep end demarcated by a diving board. Hardscaping adds pizzazz, with an expanse of concrete flagstone patio, graduated down a slight slope from the residence. *Courtesy of Terry Pool Company, Inc.*

A spa creates a watery side bar to this classic rectangular pool. Steps emphasize the shallow end's corners. The entire project is outlined in brick retaining wall, and underlined in slate flagstones. *Courtesy of Maryland Pools, Inc.*

© Alan Gilbert Photography

A fascinating blend of natural and nature's opposite — an even slice of perfect rectangle — create contrast in a green expanse bordered by soft-edged landscaping. *Courtesy of Aqua-Qual Swimming Pool Co.*

Little extras add luxury to basic design — an inset hot tub and a guide for lap swimmers. Beyond, an engineering feat in concrete holds back a hillside and creates a comfortable path to the swimming spot. *Courtesy of Klimat Master Pools*

Graduating in size, a spa and pool point toward a lakeside view. The spa spillover creates a four-foot waterfall. *Courtesy of Olympic Pools & Spas*

The perfect symmetry of a rectangular swimming hole is softened at the edges by broken landscaping — an abstract extension of marble-white stone amidst a sea of green grass. *Courtesy of Mission Pools*

A half-moon spa adds punctuation to this exclamation mark of a pool, set in a warm nest of slate-gray pavers. *Courtesy of Rizzo Pool Construction Co.*

A black plaster dye adds mystery to the depths, and intrigue to the garden. *Courtesy of Sun & Swim Pools, Inc.*

Hardscaping frames an elegant black pool, adorning its shores with garden walls, a raised spa, and a stone fireplace. *Courtesy of High-Tech Pools, Inc.*

Submerged stools create seating in this cool and classic retreat, where a waterfall adds amazing impact. *Courtesy of Shasta Pools & Spas*

A landing pushes its way into a sleek slash of pool. The brief peninsula creates a patio in a spare setting of hardscaping and swim space. *Courtesy of Aqua Blue Pools*

Bubbles give away an otherwise disguised spa, integral to the pool. *Courtesy of Gib-San Pools, Ltd.*

An arch creates an inviting entryway into the shallow end of a sparkly blue pool, set in a foot-friendly wood deck. *Courtesy of Aqua Blue Pools*

Scallops into or out of a rectangle pool are typical design adaptations to the classic rectangular pool. *Courtesy of Patio Pools of Tucson, Inc.*

A pool points arrow-like at falling water. Beyond, a spa bubbles invitingly. *Courtesy of Sun & Swim Pools, Inc.*

A rectangle is modified with an El that includes an incorporated spa and a soothing fountain spill from a raised beam. *Courtesy of Hollandia Pools & Spas*

A vanishing edge terminates a series of levels and side-trips for a free-flowing assembly of straight lines. Contained within this assortment or eye-teasing lines are a spa and a lap lane, along with great nooks where one can rest and take in the seaside view. *Courtesy of Aqua-Qual Swimming Pool Co.*

A variety of levels add interest to pool and spa. Minimalist landscaping creates minimal upkeep. *Courtesy of Shasta Pools & Spas*

A corner of private garden becomes home to a cool black-lined pool, surrounded by soft landscaping. *Courtesy of Gib-San Pools, Ltd.*

Spa, wading area, and a deep end sparkled by water fountains are united in underwater lighting magic. The easy assembly of shapes belies the underpinnings of concrete retaining walls that make this all possible on a steeply sloped lot. *Courtesy of Shasta Pools & Spas*

A shady pavilion invites swimmers to dry on the far side of a pool. If they've just soaked in the spa, it's but a short swim away across cooler waters. *Courtesy of Geremia Pools, Inc.*

A pool shadows the shape of the impressive home beyond, working as an extension of the architecture. *Courtesy of Lombardo Swimming Pool Co.*

A pool creates a dramatic centerpiece for a courtyard, bordered on two sides by home, another by classic pavilion. *Courtesy of Artistic Pools, Inc.*

Opposite page: Perfectly symmetrical, an elegant pool doubles as reflecting pond for the amazing home beyond. *Courtesy of Artistic Pools, Inc.*

Circles and squares merge, creating a blue gemstone in this small patio space. *Courtesy of Southwest Pools & Spas*

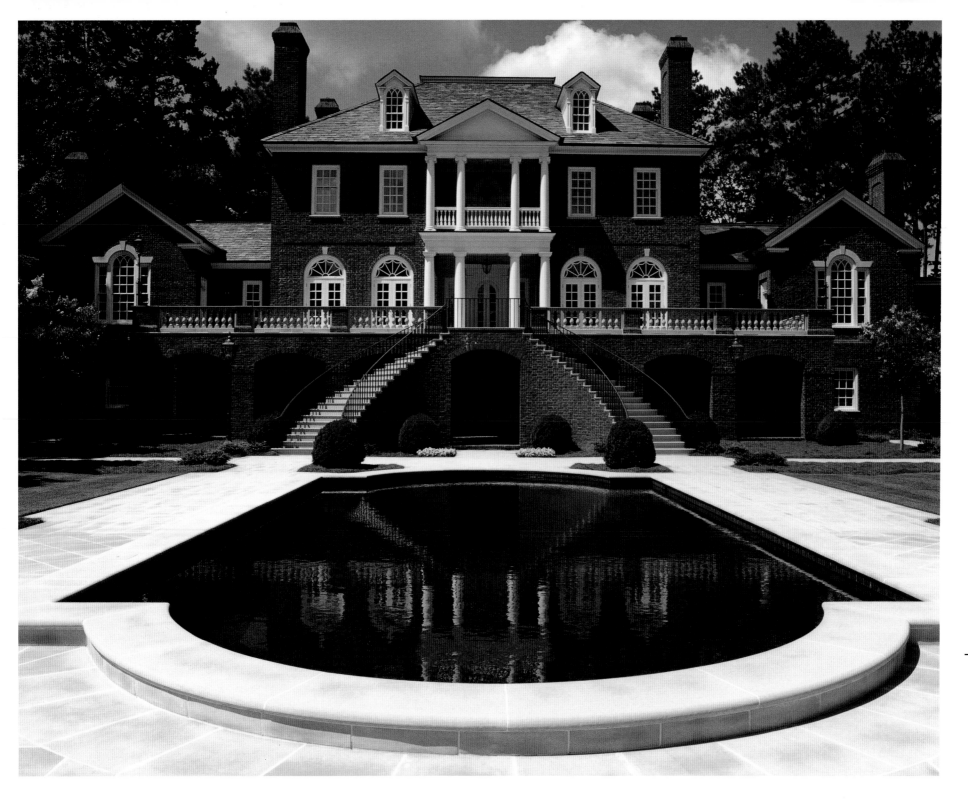

Neo-Classical

Roman baths once defined the height of Western culture. The columns and arches that defined Roman architecture set the standard for elegance in today's architectural projects.

Stately columns and an overflowing urn evoke a Roman bath. *Courtesy of Hurst Gunite Pools*

Decorative only, these columns evoke an aura of ancient elegance. *Courtesy of Terry Pool Company, Inc.*

Lion-head fountains and handled planters are excellent reproductions of pool ornamentation enjoyed by ancient Italians. Two thoughtful gargoyles are nice touches as well. If the stone faces don't distract you, you may notice the vanishing edge at the far side of the raised pool — an enchanting ending to a stone space, complete with the sound of flowing water. *Courtesy of Shasta Pools & Spas*

Lion-head fountains and planters were used to create symmetry and style around a spacious pool. *Courtesy of Curtis Pools*

A wall of travertine elevates the spa/fountain on the far side of the pool, while evoking classic Italian tile work. Note that a ledge follows the wall just under the water line — a safety precaution as well as an inviting perch. The entryway to the pool is an expansive, child-friendly wading area covered in a travertine design. *Courtesy of Geremia Pools, Inc.*

Classic features surround a classically shaped pool. An elevated spa overlooks the whole scene. *Courtesy of Mission Pools*

An elevated edge adds opportunity for display. Here a handsome little pool creates a shadow to the home. Setting the concrete grid at an angle to the home creates an illusion of greater patio space. *Courtesy of Artistic Pools, Inc.*

Balance and symmetry characterize this elegant pool, gracefully centered by a spill-over spa.
Courtesy of The Clearwater Company, Inc.

Opposite page: A little courtyard display creates a corner of classic elegance.
Courtesy of Pool Builders, Inc.

Contemporary Flair

Here are daring designs for those willing to take forward leaps in aesthetics. Each is as exciting as it is unique.

A curved expanse of pool spills over a polished edge, all in black — perfect contrast to the sleek white home beyond and a stunning structure in its own right. *Courtesy of Mission Pools*

Wandering patio and pool create a walking garden indicative of Japanese Zen gardens. In the far corner, an outdoor fireplace adds contrasting appeal to the cool blue of the water. *Courtesy of Artistic Pools, Inc.*

Strong walls were erected in a major landscaping project that created a flat area for home and sport. Half circles define pool, house, and built-in seating around a circular fire pit. *Courtesy of Pool Tech Midwest, Inc.*

High drama is created in arrow-like pool shape, S-curved steps. and a far wall of fountains, including a spray that rises from the spa. *Courtesy of Sandler Pools*

Small but sweet, this artistically crafted pool was created with leisure in mind. A half wall at the far side invites soakers to linger, head on arms, while taking in a view of the golf course beyond. *Courtesy of Artistic Pools, Inc.*

These proud pool owners can survey their swimming hole from a perch atop a waterfall. Below, cooling waters and a soothing spa beckon. *Courtesy of Aqua Blue Pools*

Angles in walls and pool mirror the roof line overhead. Besides a hot spot for soaking, sunken chairs surround an in-pool table. *Courtesy of Aqua Blue Pools*

Wood warms the edges of a dramatic black pool, where trees and trellis are reflected. *Courtesy of Arrow Master Pools*

Stepping stones invite one to cross a cool black pool, where your reflection awaits. A lap pool beyond calls for more vigorous introspection. *Courtesy of Alka Pool Construction, Ltd.*

Falling waters skirt a home, creating swimming and wading space, as well as the soothing sounds of water on the move. *Courtesy of Mission Pools*

Water slips over the far edge of a pool, creating a soft edge that opens the view for swimmers in this raised pool. *Courtesy of Mission Pools*

Nautilus-like, a wall shelters spa waters from the sweep of swim space beyond. *Courtesy of Mission Pools*

Short on space, particularly flat space, this pool manages to be both a small lap pool and a water feature for its owners. *Courtesy of Memphis Pool Supply Co.*

Free-Style

Today's hottest trend in pool design is to make it look as though Mother Nature designed it herself. Pools are given soft, curved edges that meander within a landscape. The results are remarkable.

Pond-like, a pool is allowed to puddle amidst a generous concrete skirt. *Courtesy of Artistic Pools, Inc.*

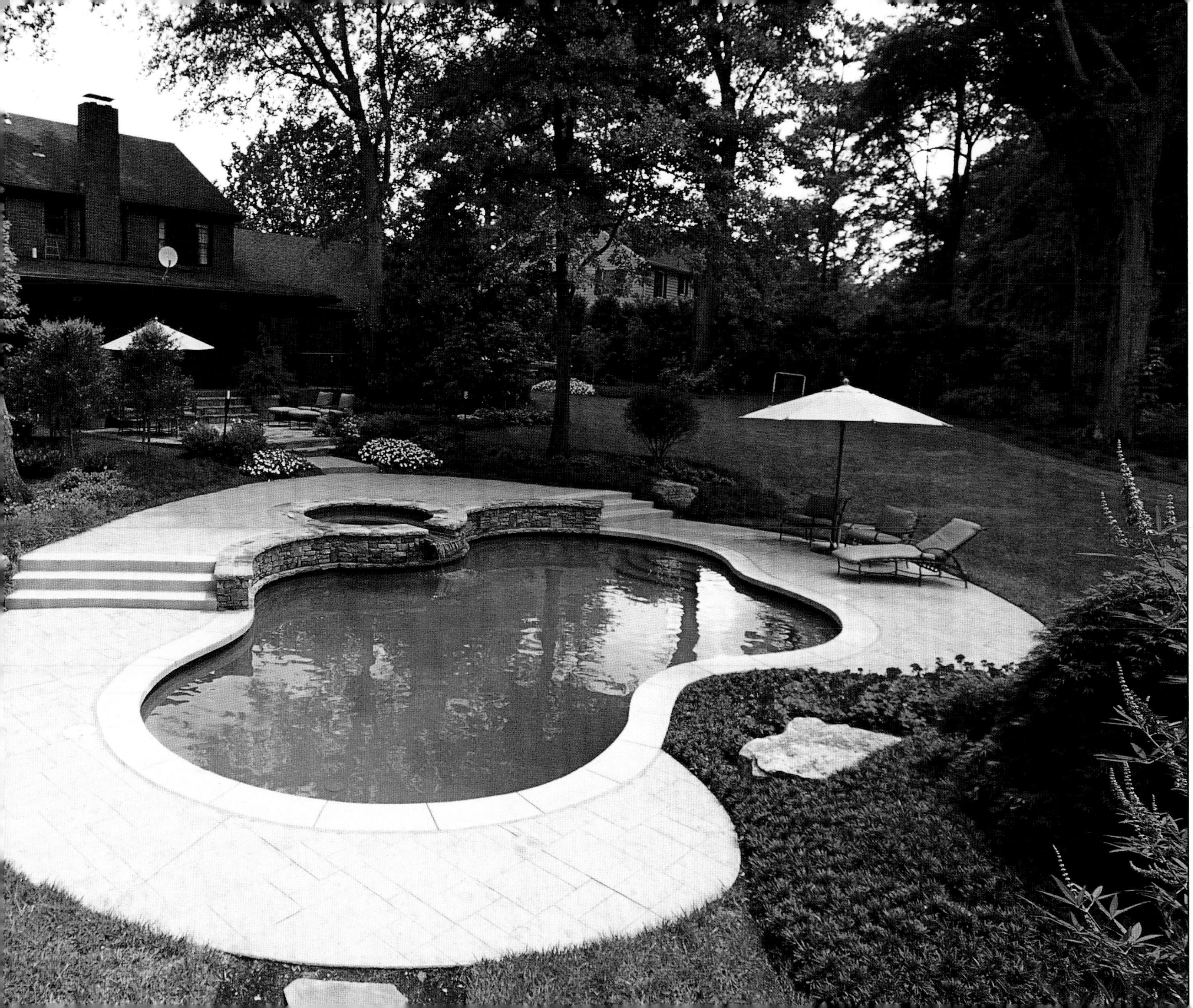

A kidney-bean shaped pool like this one raised eyebrows, and headlines, in 1948. The design by Thomas Church has been much imitated since. *Courtesy of Klimat Master Pools*

A series of curves wends its way around an inviting blue dip. *Courtesy of Memphis Pool Supply Co.*

44

A bridge arches over a natural-edge pool, creating a divider between spa and the cooler waters beyond. *Courtesy of London Pool & Spa, Inc.*

45

A man-made pool and waterfall precede the perfect swimming hole beyond. *Courtesy of Beattie Master Pool & Spa*

Natural stone retaining walls and a pile of boulders create the impression that this pool was a gift from Mother Nature. *Courtesy of Maryland Pools, Inc.*

47

Creative concrete stones create stepping stones both around and within this free-flowing swimming pool, linked by a bridge to a putting green. *Courtesy of Patio Pools of Tucson, Inc.*

Decorative concrete work skirts a pool and color-keys with the home beyond. Boulders break up the smooth edge of the pool and add awe to the overall effect. *Courtesy of Sandler Pools*

A free-flowing edge offers all manner of entry points for a swimmer approaching from the house, while a straight line defines the far terminus. *Courtesy of Shasta Pools & Spas*

A pool seems to have simply run its own pattern away from a straight starting point near the home. A flagstone deck accommodates it, and a circular spa. *Courtesy of Hollandia Pools & Spas*

A spa steams next to a cool pool, surrounded by a radiating pattern of concrete pavers.
Courtesy of Gib-San Pools, Ltd.

51

Whimsical

Here are a few examples of pure and simple fun in planning and design. After all, what is a pool for if not for fun?

A pool with sole, this one leaves a lasting impression. *Courtesy of Meredith Swimming Pool Co.*

A sea turtle outline adds aquatic interest to this oval pool. *Courtesy of Aqua Blue Pools*

Angles create drama in this sharp little pool that incorporates a wading area and a deeper dip, intersected by a circular spa. *Courtesy of Mission Pools*

An exaggerated four-leaf clover forms a memorable centerpiece for a backyard. *Courtesy of The Clearwater Company, Inc.*

A colorful pool deck forms a fancy frame for a free-form pool. *Courtesy of Curtis Pools*

55

A note of whimsy completes a pool, with a long lap lane, a semi-circular entry, and another half circle where one might choose to rest in the water. *Courtesy of Gym & Swim*

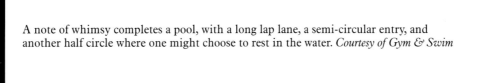

A tiled dividing wall between spa and pool imitates ivory keys. *Courtesy of Madison Swimming Pool Co., Inc.*

Focal Points

Any fine artist or designer will tell you that the key to good design is to create a focal point, a dominant landmark in an overall look. Here pavilions, waterfalls, statuary, and other elements illustrate ways to give your pool just such a central conversation piece.

Without a shade shelter set on a far corner, you'd have a flat expanse of rectangular pool and white skirt. *Courtesy of Vaughan Pools & Spas*

Statuary forms a delicate point-of-interest at the far end of a pool, watching over a semi-circular vanishing edge. *Courtesy of High-Tech Pools, Inc.*

A prancing statue invites you to follow him to a pavilion in the distance. *Courtesy of High-Tech Pools, Inc.*

A pyramid of steps seems to emerge from the greenery, and offers a stair-stepping waterfall for focal distraction and sound effects. *Courtesy of Mission Pools*

A dramatic backdrop was fashioned in tile and stone, an attractive setting where the pool is front and center. *Courtesy of Mission Pools*

Opposite page: A pavilion can also form a gathering place, here sheltering a spa beside a sparkly blue pool. *Courtesy of Riverbend Pools*

A mound of rock forms a waterfall and shelters the adjacent spa. *Courtesy of Aqua Blue Pools*

Opposite page: Water fountains and a pavilion create a show to entertain and cool sunbathers. *Courtesy of Riverbend Pools*

A rock waterfall is part of a raised platform, an inviting place to survey pool and patio, or to soak in the spa. *Courtesy of Maryland Pools, Inc.*

© Alan Gilbert Photography

A towering stand of rocks spills fresh water into a pool, flanked by an amazing assembly of quarried stone wall and patio. *Courtesy of Olympic Pools & Spas*

A spa doubles as water fountain shadowed by a classic pavilion beyond. *Courtesy of Riverbend Pools*

Four columns flank a spa, adding stature without impeding a watery view. *Courtesy of Hurst Gunite Pools*

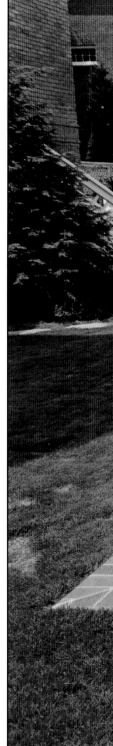

Opposite page: A pavilion is mirrored in a black-bottomed reflecting pool, which also doubles as lap pool. *Courtesy of Artistic Pools, Inc.*

Top: Columns support a trellis that adds partial shade to an elevated spa, and a classic balustrade rail transports the visitor far from this simple cornfield setting. *Courtesy of Master Pools by Paul Haney, Inc.*

Bottom: Two towers add light effects by night, water drama around the clock. *Courtesy of Geremia Pools, Inc.*

Garden Centerpieces

Like a garden pond (except you'll want to swim in it) these lovely little pools are the blue gems of their caretaker's Eden.

Though you might think to swim in it, this pool performs as a gem in a lushly landscaped backyard.
Courtesy of Riverbend Pools

A small yard is packed with foliage, setting for a bright aqua gem. *Courtesy of Gib-San Pools, Ltd.*

Slate surrounds a pretty garden pool, where fountains splash and soothe an atmosphere rich in carefully tended blooms. *Courtesy of Pool Tron*

A cozy backyard gains privacy from a screen of shady foliage. Set dead center in a flagstone patio, an oval pool reflects the leafy overhang. *Courtesy of Aqua Blue Pools*

Black-eyed Susans and wildflowers set the stage for a free-style pool, carved out amidst a loose boundary of boulders and concrete skirting. *Courtesy of Madison Swimming Pool Co., Inc.*

Formal flower and herb beds outline a rectangular pool, haven for a gardener and respite from her hot work. *Courtesy of Gib-San Pools, Ltd.*

This inviting swimming pool beckons dippers to stroll across a large, landscaped lawn to reach its shores. *Courtesy of Medallion Pools*

Shrubbery and flowers create texture and color around a symmetrical pool. *Courtesy of Medallion Pools*

Formal shape and a trio of fountains incorporate this pool into the formal landscaping of its surroundings. *Courtesy of Sandler Pools*

An expanse of patio and pool terminates in shade and foliage, a green counterbalance to sun-friendly activities. *Courtesy of Memphis Pool Supply Co.*

Opposite page: An idyllic pool is surrounded by a balanced ratio of hard and soft scaping. *Courtesy of Memphis Pool Supply Co.*

Trees above, wood below create a warm blanket for bathers, surrounded by greenery. *Courtesy of Arrow Master Pools*

A gardener's dearest projects are kept close at hand by a jewel of a
swimming pool and spa, set on a large lot. *Courtesy of High-Tech Pools, Inc.*

A clean expanse of pavers creates a barrier between the pool environment and an abundance of foliage within this compact backyard paradise. *Courtesy of Memphis Pool Supply Co.*

Flagstone trail meanders past flowerbeds and opens on a small pool and raised spa. *Courtesy of Artistic Pools, Inc.*

A black bottom, extra-wide lap lane create a beautiful reflecting pool within a formal garden setting. *Courtesy of Aqua Blue Pools*

A garden shed doubles as pool house in this intimate backyard Eden. *Courtesy of Gib-San Pools, Ltd.*

Like ancient Roman courtyards, a small pool doubles as cool dip and a central water source for the lush flowers that flank it. *Courtesy of Aqua Blue Pools*

Lion-head fountains and blue tile underline a planter lush with greenery. *Courtesy of Memphis Pool Supply Co.*

A gardener concentrates her efforts around a delicate wrought-iron fence, where cool waters wait to refresh her. *Courtesy of Gib-San Pools, Ltd.*

Natural rock edging and plantings chosen from nature's palette create an integral setting for swimming. *Courtesy of Barrington Pools, Inc.*

Small Yards & Little Dips

A small pool can be as refreshing as a big one, and may be more practical for your needs, or your space. Here are wonderful examples where a lot was made with a little.

The bulk of a brief backyard is dedicated to swimming, but there's still a little room for roses and other ornamentals beyond the pool's skirt.
Courtesy of Gib-San Pools, Ltd.

The common instinct in surrounding a pool is to create privacy. But stockade fencing and towering hedges tend to make a small yard feel stifling.
Here open fencing and soft shrubbery define the periphery, without closing out the light and view. *Courtesy of Memphis Pool Supply Co.*

Ornamental fencing and plantings add window dressing to a sparkly blue pool. *Courtesy of Memphis Pool Supply Co.*

Underwater lighting in pool and spa create an intimate outdoor space. *Courtesy of Shasta Pools & Spas*

93

A lap pool built for exercise and fitness compliments this foothills home. The pool features built-in seating, a spa, fireplace, and planting areas. *Courtesy of Patio Pools of Tucson, Inc.*

An interesting melange of shapes and textures — from a free-style pool to cut stone patio and fieldstone fountain, to octagonal platforms of decking — add interest and depth to a small yet multi-purpose outdoor environment. *Courtesy of Gib-San Pools, Ltd.*

Circular shapes in pool, planters, and spa add visual interest to a brief, rectangular back-yard space. *Courtesy of Master Pools by Paul Haney, Inc.*

A rock fountain faces the residence and creates a natural transition to the greenery beyond. Square pavers stones intermingle with smaller pavers around the pool and then break away to smooth the transition to green lawn. *Courtesy of Gib-San Pools, Ltd.*

A tidy pool environment is defined by neat squares of skirt, carefully potted plants, and just-so rows of trees and shrubbery in the distance. *Courtesy of Shasta Pools & Spas*

Having little yard to work with, these homeowners opted to forego lawn and dedicate the space to an elegant pool. A black lining creates a reflecting pond for the architecture overlooking it. *Courtesy of Cookes Pools and Spas*

A small pool doubles as a contemplative retreat, a private space where one can bask in the dancing light on sparkling waters, and watch the butterflies flit beyond. *Courtesy of Gib-San Pools, Ltd.*

Shape and texture add stature to this inviting backyard. Stepping stones lead to a slip-over spa. *Courtesy of Shasta Pools & Spas*

A triangular pool is sheltered neatly into the El of a towering home. *Courtesy of Rainey Pool Company*

Figure-eight curves in the pool soften the rectangular perimeters of a fenced and walled backyard. *Courtesy of Geremia Pools, Inc.*

Opposite page: A garden wall doubles as pool retaining wall and fountain in this attractive backyard setting. *Courtesy of Keith Zars Pools*

A handsome privacy fence cuts a corner and creates a concealed place for pool pump and equipment. *Courtesy of Gib-San Pools, Ltd.*

A towering shade shelter and spa anchor a symmetrical little pool, creating a picture-perfect backyard swim space. *Courtesy of New Bern Pool*

A vanishing edge marks a steep slope in the property beyond. The raised pool platform affords its occupants an excellent view. *Courtesy of Aqua Blue Pools*

Working within an existing courtyard, the creators carved out a free-style pool and a series of radiating pavers to add texture and form to the space. *Courtesy of JABCO, Inc. Master Pools*

Small peninsulas project into the yard-filling pool, creating additional seating space and an opportunity for shade. *Courtesy of Aqua Blue Pools*

A small pool and fountain add sight and sound to a small courtyard. *Courtesy of JABCO, Inc. Master Pools*

A spa invites the weary to journey to the far end of an expansive pool for a warm soak. *Courtesy of Meredith Swimming Pool Co.*

Sheltering walls surround paving and stone-lined flowerbeds, adding up to easy maintenance both around and within the pool. *Courtesy of JABCO, Inc. Master Pools*

A semi-circular spa caps a straight stretch of cool pool. *Courtesy of Gib-San Pools, Ltd.*

Contrasting stone outlines the pool and adds flair to the shape, color to the surroundings in this clean courtyard setting. *Courtesy of JABCO, Inc. Master Pools*

Limited in width by a steep bank beyond, this pool stretches out for a lap swimmer's enjoyment. *Courtesy of Gib-San Pools, Ltd.*

Every inch of yard is used here, with seating on the grass, both on chairs and the walls of a raised flower beds, skirting, and an artful stretch of cool and hot waters. *Courtesy of Artistic Pools, Inc.*

In contrast to the more wild spaces beyond, a pool area is defined by squares in flagstone and forms. *Courtesy of Arrow Master Pools*

A steep hillside beyond spills into the pool via a rock-lined waterfall. The pool is fashioned to imitate natural pond. *Courtesy of Mission Pools*

Flagstones and natural forms create a pond-like appearance for this swimming hole. *Courtesy of Mission Pools*

A free-form pool and flagstone patio share short space with
grass and plantings. *Courtesy of Gib-San Pools, Ltd.*

A free-form edge creates nooks and special seating areas in this small pool. *Courtesy of Barrington Pools, Inc.*

A waterfall and rock forms soften a small yard area dominated by hardscaping and clear blue waters. *Courtesy of Sandler Pools*

Warm aggregate skirting breaks into expansive blocks that artfully define stepping and seating areas from the lawn's greenery. *Courtesy of Master Pools by Paul Haney, Inc.*

Lap of Luxury

Physical therapists can wax poetic about the advantages of exercising in the water. We prefer to dwell on the aesthetic value possible with the merest sliver of pool.

An enclosed lap pool allows exercise all year long.
Courtesy of Artistic Pools, Inc.

Creating a garden border and a splashy edge to the patio, this lap pool also includes a central stair-step entry and waterfall. *Courtesy of Curtis Pools*

Brickwork, a wall-long waterfall, and statuary artfully disguise the practical nature of this lap pool. *Courtesy of Master Pools by Paul Haney, Inc.*

Widened to two lanes twelve feet wide, a lap pool serves for both exercise and a serviceable party pool. *Courtesy of Hollandia Pools & Spas*

Black bottom adds art and mystery to this garden pool, which doubles as a lap lane for a fitness buff. *Courtesy of Aqua Blue Pools*

A sundial times the workout in this dark stretch of cool exercise pool. *Courtesy of Meredith Swimming Pool Co.*

A privacy fence conceals a workout space. *Courtesy of Memphis Pool Supply Co.*

If the owners never entered for another lap, the money spent on this pool wouldn't be wasted. Raised above a sloping lot, with a vanishing edge on the far side, this artful stretch of sparkly blue is as much ornament as recreational object. *Courtesy of Mission Pools*

A roof and four walls allow therapeutic workouts year-round. *Courtesy of Meredith Swimming Pool Co.*

Widening a portion of this lap pool opens it up for family activities as well as fitness pursuits. *Courtesy of Gib-San Pools, Ltd.*

A lap lane strikes out on its own, working its way up a side yard, skirting the spa. *Courtesy of Alka Pool Construction, Ltd.*

An automatic cover keeps a lap pool clean and warm in this shady side yard. *Courtesy of Klimat Master Pools*

Oases

A sight for sore eyes, even amidst a lush lawn, here are miniature Paradises that beckon you to slip out of your cares and immerse yourself in healing waters.

Like a wandering camels dream, this cool pool invites amidst rock, waterfall, fountains, and steamy spa. *Courtesy of Paradise Pools & Spas*

Palms and gas tiki lamps complete the impression that one has arrived at an idyllic blue lagoon. *Courtesy of Shasta Pools & Spas*

Opposite page: Cactus and rock flank an aqua expanse of free-style pool and spa. *Courtesy of Patio Pools of Tucson, Inc.*

Man created the running streams, and chlorine makes the catch basin safe and clean for swimming. *Courtesy of Custom Pools, Inc.*

A waterfall completes the impression that one has arrived at a natural swimming hole, but smooth concrete skirting on the near side, and a foot-friendly bottom make it friendly to human visitors. *Courtesy of Paradise Pools & Spas*

Concrete has been fashioned to mimic a stone ledge, containing a cool blue pool and a bubbling hot spa. Lush foliage adds a natural privacy screen to this mini Eden. *Courtesy of Paradise Pools & Spas*

A tri-cornered pool fills a white concrete skirt, surrounded by greenery and more natural stone hardscaping including a waterfall. *Courtesy of Vaughan Pools & Spas*

At the foot of a green mountain, fieldstone and black-bottom pool invite swimmers and sunbathers. A pool house provides refreshment and rest areas. *Courtesy of Maryland Pools, Inc.*

129

Turtle-like, sunbathers can clamber up on a rock within the pool and warm themselves before slipping back into the cool water. *Courtesy of Vaughan Pools & Spas*

Curving palms complement the curves of a free-form pool. *Courtesy of Pool Builders, Inc.*

A natural rock edge softens the curvilinear shape of a backyard oasis, complete with hot spa. *Courtesy of Gib-San Pools, Ltd.*

Stone hardscaping adds natural flair to the skirting of a free-style pool. Soft landscaping throughout the remainder of the yard adds to the natural effect. *Courtesy of Rizzo Pool Construction Co.*

Each of three curvy extensions of this charming pool points to the lagoon beyond. A flagstone path extends from the patio to the larger waterway beyond. *Courtesy of Panama Pools of N.W. Florida*

An enormous manmade pond sits 15 feet higher than the lake beyond, affording swimmers an amazing view. *Courtesy of Maryland Pools, Inc.*

A vanishing edge allows an unobstructed view of the river beyond. *Courtesy of Custom Pools, Inc.*

Dynamite was necessary in order to create this seaside pool. Decking creates a soft environment for the human swimmers. *Courtesy of Gib-San Pools, Ltd.*

Blue waters meander amidst palms. *Courtesy of Pools by LaGasse*

135

Waterscapes

Masterworks of master planning, here are pools that integrate with patios and landscapes. The result is a complete package that urges house dwellers to leave their roofs behind.

A watery playground stretches on, flowing from a waterfall and sliding board below a far pavilion and squeezing between flower beds toward a pool closer to the home. *Courtesy of New Bern Pool*

A extensive wonderland, a pool house offers respite from the sun while an enormous pool and surrounding patio and pathways beckon one out. *Courtesy of Gym & Swim*

A bridge invites all generations to cross, where a pavilion offers a gossip center for the adults while a playground calls for the kids. *Courtesy of Gib-San Pools, Ltd.*

A manmade stream pours into a swimming area, and gurgles out the other side. *Courtesy of New Bern Pool*

Fire and water exist side-by-side in a rocky environment that evokes a natural paradise. The waterfall doubles as a slide for a quick exit from the warm spa. *Courtesy of Mission Pools*

© Eric Auerbach

Massive equipment was used to create this boulder-lined environment, which promises to long outlive its occupants. *Courtesy of Creative Master Pools*

© Eric Auerbach

Jets arc out over the pool, making the surface dance and providing a show. *Courtesy of Mission Pools*

Cooking area and a fireplace overlook a sparkly blue desert gem. *Courtesy of Shasta Pools & Spas*

A bird's-eye perspective offers a peep into the bench-seating spa, tube slide, and a meander-ing pool that includes a wading area for children. *Courtesy of Creative Master Pools*

A rushing waterfall forms the headwaters for an extensive family recreation area spread around sparkly blue water. *Courtesy of Southwest Pools & Spas*

Soft curves point the way to the woods beyond. Closer to home, flagstone and columned shade shelter offer friendly habitat. *Courtesy of New Bern Pool*

143

Free-style form in pool and patio create an inviting backyard destination. *Courtesy of Rizzo Pool Construction Co.*

Underwater seating is defined by black tile squares. A spill-over spa faces back toward the house. *Courtesy of Klimat Master Pools*

A bridge cordons off a private swim spot, complete with waterfall. A delightful destination for lovers and giggly children alike. *Courtesy of Gib-San Pools, Ltd.*

Extensive stone skirting around a free-form pool makes a statement in an extensive yard.
Courtesy of Rizzo Pool Construction Co.

A family focuses on the pool, even in the house. The walkout basement opens onto the patio, and the ground floor extends into a broad balcony. *Courtesy of Rizzo Pool Construction Co.*

A cozy corner pool seems to be an extension of the foothill beyond, with a mountain stream spilling over rocks into the swimming area. Steps lead to a spa, that can be hot and ready with an hour's notice. *Courtesy of Mission Pools*

An extension of the home makes it possible to step into the spa without venturing any further outdoors. Just beyond, a pool shadows the home behind, creating a sheltered swimming and patio area. *Courtesy of Artistic Pools, Inc.*

Three water features have been packaged into a pretty backyard gem — pool, spa, and semi-circular water fountain. *Courtesy of Artistic Pools, Inc.*

A black finish on an L-shaped pool and slip-over-spa creates pleasing contrast with warm gray and white paving. A gardener's blooms are expertly framed within the manmade environment. *Courtesy of Mission Pools*

Topiary adds punctuation to a lawn and pool designed with symmetry and harmony as key ingredients. *Courtesy of Artistic Pools, Inc.*

A rock wall gives way to a 25-foot waterfall into a manmade pool that spills over a semi-circular smooth edge and recycles. The pool was cut into a cliff with a diamond-studded chain saw. Rock steps were built into the pool. The pool is nine-feet deep below the cliff to allow jumping from on top. The shallow end is located behind the cliff on the left. *Courtesy of Mowry Pools*

A spa spills over and runs under flagstone decking and into the pool beyond. *Courtesy of Hollandia Pools & Spas*

A gate opens in a delicate wrought iron fence, inviting you to a wonderland pool complete with a spa and a rock perch overlooking all. *Courtesy of Gib-San Pools, Ltd.*

153

Tiki Bars & Pool Houses

Stocked refrigerators, convenient lavatories, and any other imaginable amenity have been incorporated into these poolside hangouts.

A panel slides up and the bar is open for pool-side refreshments. Nearby, a grill is ready to cook up reinforcements. *Courtesy of Pool Tech Midwest, Inc.*

A pool house offers both privacy and adjacent shade in this nature-inspired setting. *Courtesy of Maryland Pools, Inc.*

156

The little watering hole next to the larger one has been whimsically dubbed McTiki. *Courtesy of Maryland Pools, Inc.*

An expansive screened-in porch flanks pool, spa, and lake. It's only steps to the water. *Courtesy of Lombardo Swimming Pool Co.*

157

A family's life is oriented outdoor, with an extensive deck, a poolhouse on expanse of patio, and a tennis court for more vigorous activity. *Courtesy of Gym & Swim*

Pull up a stool next to a pool-side bar. A huge picnic table accommodates large gatherings of bathers and diners. *Courtesy of Gib-San Pools, Ltd.*

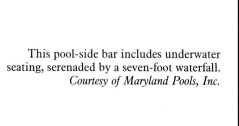

This pool-side bar includes underwater seating, serenaded by a seven-foot waterfall. *Courtesy of Maryland Pools, Inc.*

A columned shade shelter over an open-air bar and seating adds formality to a free-form pool. *Courtesy of Maryland Pools, Inc.*

A tap and fridge are at the ready for cold refreshments, and a grill is available for hot food preparation. *Courtesy of Gym & Swim*

Changing rooms and a small kitchen area share a small pool house, with shaded seating attached. *Courtesy of Gib-San Pools, Ltd.*

His and hers dressing areas stretch pool side, providing a wall of shelter and privacy for this courtyard pool. A fireplace and waterfall complete the ideal watery hangout. *Courtesy of Patio Pools of Tucson, Inc.*

A playhouse shelters the spa and offers game and changing areas inside. *Courtesy of Alka Pool Construction, Ltd.*

A small pool house blends with fencing to provide a warm flank for a cool pool and bubbling spa. *Courtesy of Gib-San Pools, Ltd.*

161

A rec room shares space with pool and spa within a double-walled yard. A sunken bar allows swimmers to belly up on underwater stools and refresh themselves. *Courtesy of Greenville Pool & Supply Co.*

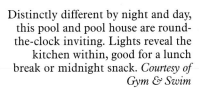

Distinctly different by night and day, this pool and pool house are round-the-clock inviting. Lights reveal the kitchen within, good for a lunch break or midnight snack. *Courtesy of Gym & Swim*

Lighting around the pool and pool house
creates an attractive, intimate environment by night. *Courtesy of Gym & Swim*

A sweet little pool house harbors supplies in a tidy, self-contained backyard. *Courtesy of Gib-San Pools, Ltd.*

165

Soft furnishings invite interior lounging pool side for those who shun the sun. A vanishing edge terminates the elevated pool area in a soft waterfall. *Courtesy of Rizzo Pool Construction Co.*

167

Brick and iron contain a complete play area, including changing facilities and cooking areas in a handsome pool house. *Courtesy of Burleson Pool Company*

Tile and blond brick add Mediterranean flavor to a luxurious pool environment.
Courtesy of Greenville Pool & Supply Co.

169

Fire and Water

Two elements that don't mix by nature – fire and water – work well side by side in these settings. A fireplace takes the chill off a cool evening, and helps warm a drying body poolside. The result is an opportunity to linger longer outdoors.

A chimenea or pre-fab fireplace are excellent and easy options for creating a warm spot next to your cool one. *Courtesy of Artistic Pools, Inc.*

Extra stone was obtained from the patio project and used to build an attractive stone fireplace, which provides both warmth on a cool evening, and an attractive focal point pool side. *Courtesy of Artistic Pools, Inc.*

A stone columned pavilion shelters a cooking
fire. *Courtesy of Shasta Pools & Spas*

173

An extension of the home, this attached pavilion overhangs an outdoor barbecue. *Courtesy of Shasta Pools & Spas*

A massive fireplace was built as part of an outdoor living environment. *Courtesy of Keith Zars Pools*

A stucco fireplace is part of the wall sheltering this desert oasis. *Courtesy of Patio Pools of Tucson, Inc.*

Old World charm is created in a timelessly appealing environment of rock, water, and fire. *Courtesy of Prestige Pools & Spas*

Tricks of the Trade

Here are a few of the really "wow" features today's Master Pool Builders can incorporate into a pool environment. Besides making pools safer and more aesthetically pleasing, these features may simply make a pool possible in wooded or sloped lots that might otherwise be unwelcoming to a clean swimming environment.

Gradual Entry

A sloped entry into deeper waters serves several purposes. It's more child friendly, creating a greater area where they can play, and provides handicapped access as well as an added safety factor for poor swimmers or pets that fall in accidentally.

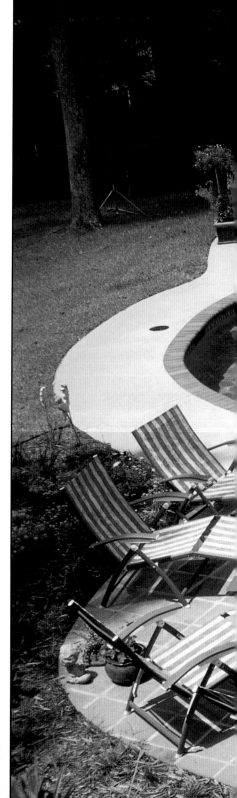

Blue stone inlay marks a pool entryway. *Courtesy of Pro Pools & Spas*

A natural-looking lagoon includes a beach-like entry. *Courtesy of Klimat Master Pools*

A sloped entryway counterbalances a spa on the other side. *Courtesy of Shasta Pools & Spas*

Three easy steps lead to deeper waters, providing a toddler-friendly play area. *Courtesy of Rainey Pool Company*

Beach-like, a gradual entry leads to a shallow ledge, where waders and smaller people can play. *Courtesy of Shasta Pools & Spas*

For those who want to ease their way in, there's a sloped entry on the far side of the pool. *Courtesy of Shasta Pools & Spas*

A pool's black finish extends out onto the patio in a graduated entryway. *Courtesy of Klimat Master Pools*

Vanishing Edge

The drama queens of contemporary pool design, vanishing edges create an uninterrupted view across one end of a pool. Today's master pool builders can make that vanishing edge extend around multiple sides, or curve the fall-off. The water tumbles in an ear-pleasing cascade, and pools in a catch basin where it is filtered and recycled back into the pool.

When a pool becomes part of its surroundings. *Courtesy of Neuman Pools, Inc.*

Courtesy of Aqua Blue Pools

This beautiful vanishing edge pool was built on a severe slope requiring massive structural walls and footings. An elevated spa on one end overflows into the main pool and on the opposite end there is a 6" deep shelf for lounging slightly underwater. *Courtesy of Artistic Pools, Inc.*

A double waterfall, from spa to pool, and across the vanishing edge. *Courtesy of Artistic Pools, Inc.*

This vanishing edge pool with man-made boulders was built on a high hill overlooking a large river below. *Courtesy of Artistic Pools, Inc.*

A simple but elegant double vanishing edge rectangular pool that reflects the forest behind. *Courtesy of Artistic Pools, Inc.*

A rectangular vanishing edge pool with motorized cover overlooks the rolling forest below. *Courtesy of Artistic Pools, Inc.*

A bench provides seating where one can enjoy the unobstructed view afforded by a double vanishing edge. *Courtesy of Artistic Pools, Inc.*

187

This vanishing edge geometric pool overflows above the owner's putting green. *Courtesy of Artistic Pools, Inc.*

Water from the vanishing edge overflows into a trough so that it can be re-circulated back into the pool. *Courtesy of Artistic Pools, Inc.*

Courtesy of Geremia Pools, Inc.

189

Courtesy of Geremia Pools, Inc.

Courtesy of London Pool & Spa, Inc.

Courtesy of Riverbend Pools

An amazing curved vanishing edge pool with a spa and four-sided vanishing edge water feature presents a mirror smooth appearance.
Courtesy of Patio Pools of Tucson, Inc.

Courtesy of Patio Pools of Tucson, Inc.

191

Courtesy of Shasta Pools & Spas

Courtesy of Shasta Pools & Spas

A pool cascades on all sides, with access only via bridge. *Courtesy of Shasta Pools & Spas*

Courtesy of Aqua Blue Pools

193

A small double vanishing edge pool with elevated spa and beautiful blue stone decking.
Courtesy of Artistic Pools, Inc.

Located on the eastern brow of Lookout Mountain, this pool features a 12-foot waterfall. From deck level, the pool appears to flow into the City of Chattanooga beyond. *Courtesy of JABCO, Inc. Master Pools*

Courtesy of Mission Pools

197

An enormous waterfall creates an explosion of sound below a peaceful expanse of cool blue pool and spa. *Courtesy of Prestige Pools & Spas*

Water Towers

A steeply sloped lot can't stop an expert pool builder. Heavy equipment, sunken supports, and retaining walls can conquer all. The result is a watery perch with incredible views. And the ability to soak where one might only slide before.

Courtesy of Aqua Blue Pools

199

A grotto beckons lovers. *Courtesy of Rizzo Pool Construction Co.*

200

This hillside setting is complete with a negative-edge pool and wooden catwalk, approximately 18 feet high. *Courtesy of Gib-San Pools, Ltd.*

A crescent pool overlooks an expansive lake. *Courtesy of Vaughan Pools & Spas*

A split-level pool respects the slope in this back yard.
Courtesy of Hollandia Pools & Spas

This unique tri-level pool has an upper spa that overflows into the second level and to the pool below. Beautiful limestone accents the pool and steps. *Courtesy of Artistic Pools, Inc.*

This traditional style cantilever hillside pool and spa features precast concrete coping, broken concrete stepping pads, separated with grass, and a gray plastered interior surface. *Courtesy of Symphony Pools*

Courtesy of Symphony Pools

A smooth brick face outlines the pool and
adds beauty to the retaining wall.
Courtesy of Prestige Pools & Spas

Automatic Covers

Today, the push of a button can activate an automatic cover that keeps the pool clean, the water warmer, and the surroundings safer. They're actually strong enough to walk on.

Cut rock border around the lip of this pool conceals a track where an automatic cover slides out to seal off the swimming area. *Courtesy of Olympic Pools & Spas*

Left rectangular to accommodate a cover, lower ledges add variety and interest. *Courtesy of Master Pools by Starline Pools, Inc.*

Semi-circular walls divide off spa and wading area. *Courtesy of High-Tech Pools, Inc.*

Courtesy of Terry Pool Company, Inc.

Light Show

Underwater lighting is an art form in itself, and today's masters install a changing light show that can be adjusted to reflect different needs.

A free-form pool takes on different characters day and night. *Courtesy of Gym & Swim*

Colored lights add excitement to a wonderful rock waterfall. *Courtesy of Gym & Swim*

Blue lights create underwater magic, with a shining pool house above. *Courtesy of Gym & Swim*

The dark bottom of a pool glows slightly brighter, with electric light, than the nighttime lake beyond. *Courtesy of Shasta Pools & Spas*

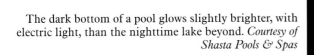

215

Lighting above ground is mandatory for safety on the stairs after dark. The underwater lighting is strictly for drama. *Courtesy of Gym & Swim*

216

Exterior lights reflect in the pool, all that's needed for magic
sparkle. *Courtesy of Gym & Swim*

Underwater lights cast an eerie glow in contrast to the night. *Courtesy of Custom Pools, Inc.*

Be it ever so humble, sunsets, clouds, and morning's early bloom may provide the best light show. Money can't buy it — you just have to be there. *Courtesy of Shasta Pools & Spas*

219

Indoor Pools

The ultimate in luxury, an indoor pool allows year-round enjoyment in any climate. No bugs, no rain or snow, and no leaves to vacuum off the bottom.

Conservatory and swimming are combined in one glorious room, with brick architecture and expansive windows that warm all with sunshine. *Courtesy of Barrington Pools, Inc.*

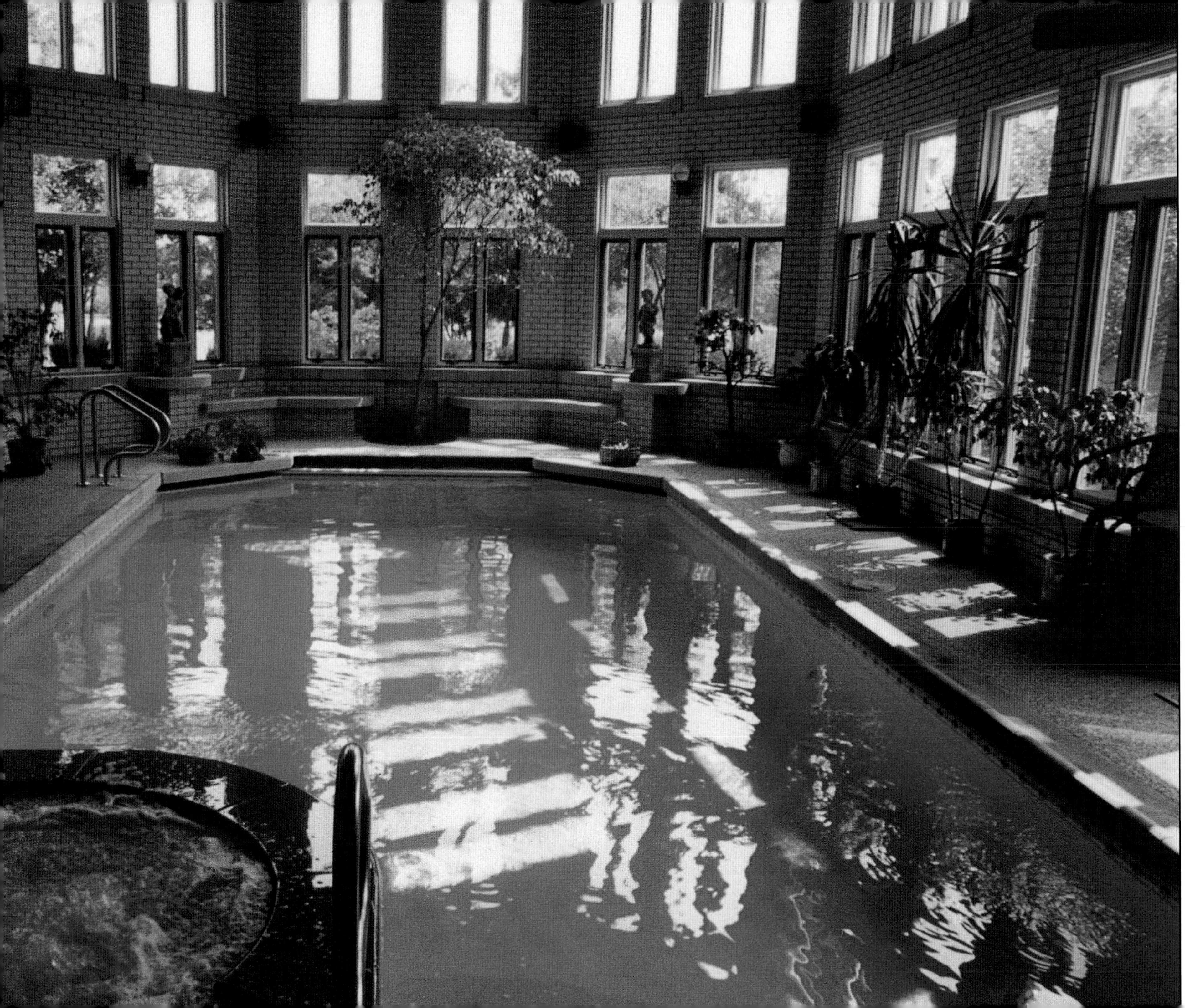

In Ontario, a pool has a limited range of usefulness outdoors, so bringing it in is well worth the investment. Here proud owners spared nothing, including nature's elements in the design — rocks and waterfalls, as well as the creature comforts of an expansive swimming area and a bubbling hot tub, all under a towering timber-frame roof. *Courtesy of Hollandia Pools & Spas*

© Andersen Photography

© Andersen Photography

223

Dedicated to sports and fitness, this pool includes two well-marked lap lanes that double as a throughway during heated basketball competition. *Courtesy of Rizzo Pool Construction Co.*

Simplicity itself, lap pool was built with one purpose in mind — fitness. *Courtesy of Alka Pool Construction, Ltd.*

Paradise under a roof, tropical plants and rock walls create a watery wonderland. *Courtesy of Gib-San Pools, Ltd.*

A family gathering place year round, this warm wooden deck is foot friendly no matter how thick the frost. *Courtesy of Aqua Blue Pools*

Weather permitting, the sliding doors open and you're practically outdoors. *Courtesy of Aqua Blue Pools*

Indoors and out, swimmers can enjoy this bright blue water under sparkling sun, or by the bar. *Courtesy of Aqua Blue Pools*

Tromp l'oil paintings create greater depth and width to an already enormous room dominated by a very large pool. *Courtesy of Gib-San Pools, Ltd.*

Hot tub and lap pool are skirted by handsome stone. *Courtesy of Barrington Pools, Inc.*

Manmade boulders add to the impression of adventure and excitement in this pool environment. *Courtesy of Gym & Swim*

Reminiscent of a ship's construction, a vaulted timber frame roof adds nautical appeal to this towering pool house.
Courtesy of Maryland Pools, Inc.

A towering conservatory channels sunlight into this handsome mosaic pool, complete with an automatic cover so that the water can be heated just so. *Courtesy of Neuman Pools, Inc.*

Enormous windows and glass block open a handsome little pool room to the watery view beyond. Inside, family and guests enjoy a sunken bar. *Courtesy of Olympic Pools & Spas*

A double spill over from spa to pool adds watery music to this newly completed pool house,

A basement level pool evokes a Roman bath, with pedestaled planters and mosaic tile trim.

A fireplace waits to warm and reinvigorate the tired lap swimmer. *Courtesy of Memphis Pool Supply Co.*

Mosaic work, hand-cut tiles, fountain heads, wrought iron, and stained glass — no expense was spared in the creation of this virtual chapel to the water gods. *Courtesy of Gib-San Pools, Ltd.*

233

Carved stone, columns and arches, and mosaic work evoke Roman elegance, and permanence. *Courtesy of Alka Pool Construction, Ltd.*

Opposite page: In Florida, glass is not necessary to keep out chilly air, but screening is generally mandated by law. The result is open air atriums shielded from minuscule pests such as mosquitoes, and bigger ones like alligators, too. *Courtesy of Florida Bonded Pools, Inc.*

The spa has been integrated as part of the pool ornament in this bright pool house addition. *Courtesy of Rizzo Pool Construction Co.*

A half wall in brick creates built-in seating and an opportunity to expose plants to the sun. Above, elegant windows make the pool house attractive both inside and out. *Courtesy of Artistic Pools, Inc.*

Skylights and sliding doors open to the outdoors in clement weather, and make one feel almost outdoors when they're closed. *Courtesy of High-Tech Pools, Inc.*

A built-in sliding board and a gradual entry make this pool room kid friendly, but who wouldn't feel like a kid again in such a paradise? *Courtesy of Gym & Swim*

A contemporary home opens on two levels to a pool house, set under a slanted glass roof. *Courtesy of Barrington Pools, Inc.*

Contributors

Master Pools® Guild, Inc.
9607 Gayton Road, Suite 200
Richmond, VA 23233
800-392-3044
www.masterpoolsguild.com

Alka Pool Construction, Ltd.
4013 Graveley Street
Burnaby, BC Canada V5C 3T5
604-320-2552
www.alkapools.com

Aqua Blue Pools
7332 Peppermill Parkway
N. Charleston, SC 29418
843-767-7665
1F Mathews Court
Hilton Head Island, SC 29926
843-689-2232
www.aquabluepools.net

Aqua-Qual Swimming Pool Company
18 Allen Boulevard
Farmingdale, NY 11735
631-293-8540
MPAquaQual@aol.com

Arrow Master Pools
4839 Route 309
Center Valley, PA 18034
800-834-0232
www.arrowmasterpools.com

Artistic Pools, Inc.
3884 N. Peachtree Road
Atlanta, GA 30341
770-458-9177
www.artisticpools.com

Barrington Pools, Inc.
PO Box 3906
Barrington, IL 60011
847-381-1245
www.barrington-pools.com

Beattie Master Pool & Spa
7760 Bay Road
Saginaw, MI 48604
989-793-7121
www.beattiemasterpool.com

Burleson Pool Company
3054 Leeman Road, Suite H
Huntsville, AL 35801
256-837-0260
www.burlesonmasterpools.com

The Clearwater Company, Inc.
1682 Lake Murray Blvd.
Columbia, SC 29212
803-781-8364
www.clearwaterco.com

Cookes Pools and Spas
PO Box 5005
Mildura, Victoria, Australia 3502
0350-221266
www.cookes.com.au

Creative Master Pools
537 Commerce Street
Franklin Lakes, NJ 07417
201-337-7600
www.creativemasterpools.com

Curtis Pools
1260 West Bay Drive, Suite F
Largo, FL 33770
727-559-7946
www.curtispools.com

Custom Pools, Inc.
4048 Chinden Blvd.
Boise, ID 83714
208-345-2792
www.custompoolsandpatio.com

Florida Bonded Pools, Inc.
8608 Beach Blvd.
Jacksonville, FL 32216
904-641-5265
www.Floridabondedpools.com

Geremia Pools, Inc.
1327 65th St.
Sacramento, CA 95819
916-227-1500
www.geremiapools.com

Gib-San Pools, Ltd.
59 Milvan
Toronto, Ontario Canada M9L 1Y8
416-749-4361
www.GibSanPools.com

Greenville Pool & Supply Company
3730 Charles Street
Greenville, NC 27858
252-355-7121
www.greenvillepool.com

Gym & Swim
8130 New LaGrange Rd.
Louisville, KY 40222
502-426-1326
www.gymandswim.com

High-Tech Pools, Inc.
31333 Industrial Parkway
Cleveland, OH 44070
440-979-5070
www.hightechpools.com

Hollandia Pools & Spas
1891 Wharncliffe Road S.
London, Ontario, Canada N6L 1K2
519-652-3257
www.hollandiagardens.com

Hurst Gunite Pools
221 Highland Circle
Trussville, AL 35173-3261
205-661-2191
www.hurstpools.com

JABCO, Inc. Master Pools
807 Missouri Street
Tuscumbia, AL 35674
256-381-2861
www.jabcopools.com

Keith Zars Pools
17427 San Pedro
San Antonio, TX 78232
210-494-0800
www.keithzarspools.com

Klimat Master Pools
PO Box 76217
Highland Heights, KY 41076
859-572-0111
www.poolsklimatmaster.com

Lifetime Pools, Inc.
910 San Antonio Road
Palo Alto, CA 94303
650-494-7070
www.lifetimepools.com

Lombardo Swimming Pool Company
1501 Industrial Drive
Matthews, NC 28105
704-847-4648
lombardopools@aol.com

London Pool & Spa, Inc.
1188 Furlong Road
Sebastopol, CA 95472
707-823-0581
www.londonpoolandspa.com

Madison Swimming Pool Company, Inc.
1416 Dickerson Road
Goodlettsville, TN 37072
615-865-2964
www.madisonpools.com

Maryland Pools, Inc.
9515 Gerwig Lane, Suite 119
Columbia, MD 21046
410-995-6600
11166 Main Street, Suite 402
Fairfax, VA 22030
703-359-7192
www.mdpools.com

Master Pools by Paul Haney, Inc.
1240 North Kelsey Street
Visalia, CA 93291
559-651-1177
www.masterpoolsvisalia.com

Master Pools by Starline Pools, Inc.
5016 Jacksboro Highway
Wichita Falls, TX 76302
940-723-7442

Medallion Pool Company
PO Box 399
Skyland, NC 28776
828-684-5381
medpoole@aol.com

Memphis Pool Supply Company
2762 Getwell Road
Memphis, TN 38118
901-365-2480
www.memphispool.com

Meredith Swimming Pool Company
116 Stagecoach Trail
Greensboro, NC 27409
336-299-7044
www.meredithpools.com

Mission Pools
755 W. Grand Avenue
Escondido, CA 92025
760-743-2605
www.missionpools.com

Mowry Pools
2108 Kippling Drive
Austin, TX 78752
512-343-1066

Neuman Pools, Inc.
W9684 Beaverland Parkway
Beaver Dam, WI 53916
800-444-0312
www.neumanpools.com

New Bern Pool
3646 Capital Blvd.
Raleigh, NC 27604
919-873-1777
www.newbernpool.com

Olympic Pools & Spas
801 Coliseum Blvd. West
Fort Wayne, IN 46808
260-482-7665
www.poolnspa.com

Panama Pools of N.W. Florida
291 Powell Adams Road
Panama City, FL 32413
850-233-0950
www.panamapoolsandspas.com

Paradise Pools & Spas
4221 Division Street
Metairie, LA 70002
504-888-0505
www.paradisepools.com

Patio Pools of Tucson, Inc.
7960 E. 22nd St.
Tucson, AZ 85710
520-886-1211
www.patiopoolsaz.com

Pool Builders, Inc.
5601 S.W. 45th Street
Davie, FL 33314
954-797-7700
www.poolbuildersinc.com

Pools by LaGasse
4559 Clark Road
Sarasota, FL 34233
941-921-4608
www.poolsbylagasse.com

Pool Tech Midwest, Inc.
3233 First Avenue S.E.
Cedar Rapids, IO 52402
319-365-8609
www.pooltech.com

Pool Tron
10403 Trenton Avenue
St. Louis, MO 63132
314-428-1971

Prestige Pools & Spas, Inc.
P.O. Box 2224
Edmond, OK 73083
405-340-7665
wedigpools@msn.com

Pro Pools & Spas
623 Romero Street
Lake Charles, LA 70607
337-477-7626
www.propools-spas.com

Rainey Pool Company
1101 Gulf Freeway
League City, TX 77573
281-338-1555
www.raineypools.com

Riverbend Pools
4016 West Plano Pkwy., Suite 100
Plano, TX 75093
972-596-7393
www.riverbendpools.com

Rizzo Pool Construction Co.
388 Stamm Road
Newington, CT 06111
860-667-2214
www.rizzopools.com

Sandler Pools
4016 W. Plano Pkwy., Suite 100
Plano, TX 75093
972-596-7393
www.sandlerpools.com

Shasta Pools & Spas
6031 North 16th Street
Phoenix, AZ 85016
602-532-3750
www.shastapools.com

Southwest Pools & Spas
8225 Buffalo Gap Road
Abilene, TX 79606
915-698-3054
www.southwestpools.com

Sun & Swim Pools, Inc.
3910 West Main Street
Grandview, MO 64030
816-761-7665
www.sunandswimpools.com

Symphony Pools
4685 Runway Street, Unit P
Simi Valley, CA 93063
805-584-9974
www.symphonypools.com

Terry Pool Company, Inc.
10350 North Michigan Road
Carmel, IN 46032
317-872-2502
www.terrypools.com

Vaughan Pools & Spas
1909 South Country Club Drive
Jefferson City, MO 65109
573-893-3650
www.vaughanpools.com